Voodoo Handbook of Cult Secrets

by

Anna Riva

Author of

Prayer Book
Powers of The Psalms
Candle Burning Magic
Devotions to The Saints
Secrets of Magical Seals
The Modern Herbal Spellbook
Modern Witchcraft Spellbook
Golden Secrets of Mystic Oils
Magic With Incense and Powders
Spellcraft, Hexcraft & Witchcraft
Voodoo Handbook of Cult Secrets
Your Lucky Number ... Forever
How to Conduct a Seance

www.indioproducts.com

INTERNATIONAL IMPORTS
236 W. MANCHESTER AVE,
LOS ANGELES, CA 90003

Reprint 1999

Occult Books - Curios - Supplies

ISBN 0-9438-3201-2

DAMBALLA
The serpent god; a symbol of the universe

CONTENTS

EZILI-FREDA: Symbol of beauty and feminine charm. She is often compared with Aphrodite of Homeric deity.

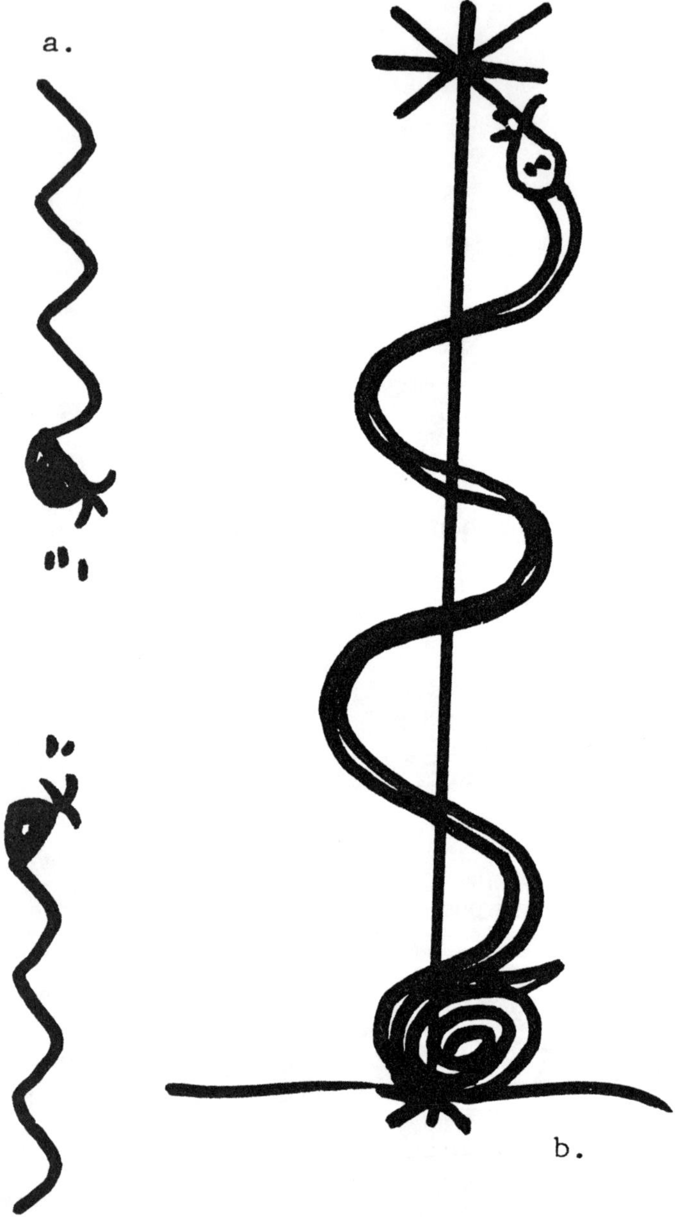

a. Ascending and descending serpents represent the ascent of the mind and incarnate thought, respectively.

b. A single serpent coiled on a staff with a star at the top represents the seven stages of initiation.

FOREWORD

Voodoo has millions of believers all over the world. It is the national, though secretly practiced for it is illegal, religion of Haiti. In New Orleans it is called "hoodoo." In Cuba and throughout South America it has various names—"santeria," "chango," "naniguismo," "candomble," and most popularly "macumba."

In English the popular spelling is voodoo, probably from the French word "vaudois" which means spirit, and "vaudou" which means introspection of the unknown.

French is the written language of Haiti, but the use of phonetics is employed by the Creole peasants in speaking—there are no grammatical rules for pronounciation.

While most Haitians today are Catholic, voodoo is practiced simultaneously by a large majority of the population. Voodoo ritual borrows heavily from Catholic services, including an altar covered with candles and surrounded by pictures of saints and the use of holy water which is sprinkled over worshipers by means of a leafy branch.

The mythology, folklore, chants and remedies of voodoo are handed down from generation to generation. Both black magic (directed towards evil ends) and white magic (concerned with easing misfortune and pain) are widely practiced, and the tools of this magic are numerous roots, herbs, oils, charms, candles, incenses, powders, essences, and other symbols which are endowed with qualities, abilities, and supernatural attributes for believers in this complex religion.

Voodoo was brought from Africa to Haiti by the enslaved Negroes, and has proved to be a constant source of comfort and hope to them. Christianity has no magic words, no power to destroy one's enemies, no evil fetishes, no promises of protection, and no cures for illness or disease. Is it any wonder then at the vast popularity of Voodoo's magical power and the eternal quest for solutions to mysterious forces?

—Anna Riva

VEVE—A symbolic geometric design which is drawn on the ground with sand, corn meal, flour, or coffee to represent the loa. There are as many different veve designs as there are various gods and spirits. Each veve is consecrated by putting on it small piles of dried foodstuff and some drink. These emblematic drawings are an important part of any ritual as they have a magical purpose—to summon the loa and to placate and honor them with food and drink.

LOA – VOODOO GODS AND DEITIES

Most names and terms for the loa are derived from old kings and gods of the Congo and Guinea, especially the African "Dahomey" people. The Creole pronunciation is phonetic, by the sound of the word and not according to any grammatical rules. There are many different styles of phonetics used.

AGAU—A storm spirit.

AGWE—Queen of heaven and earth. She is symbolized by Erzulie's boat.

AGWE-R-O-LO—Agwe's husband.

AGBETO—Two genii of the sea.

AGUASU—God of customs and traditions.

AGWE-TAROYO—The god Neptune, protector of seafaring voyagers. He is invoked under the names of "eel," "tadpole," and "sea shell."

AIZAN—Loco Attiso's wife.

ALIVODU—Guardian and protector of the house. He is symbolized by trees planted in the yards of dwellings and is invoked in the event of sickness.

ASIZA—Spirits that dwell in forests and give magical powers to man.

AYIDA-WEDO—Goddess of rain and the rainbow.

AYIZAN—Guardian goddess of paths and roads.

BADE—God of the wind.

BARON-SAMEDI—(Or Baron Cimetiere, Baron-la-Croix, or Guede Nimbo). The most feared of all loa, the Baron is of the "Guede" family and is the keeper of the cemetery. The most powerful gods cannot accomplish any spells or magic without the consent or approval of a Baron.

BRIGITTE—Baron-Samedi's wife. She has authority over ceremonial rites when the corpse is a female.

DANGBE—The supreme divinity.

DAMBALLAH—The serpent god, a symbol of the universe and one of the most important deities. He is a guardian and protector of springs, lakes, and ponds. His sacred day is Thursday, and white is his color.

DON PEDRO—A powerful voodoo priest who lived in the early days of the colony of Dahomey.

EZILI—The most famous of the female loa. A beautiful, flirtatious goddess who is the essence of voluptuous femininity. Tuesdays and Thursdays are regarded as her sacred days.

EZILI-FREDA—Goddess of beauty.

EZILI-JE-ROUGE—"Red-eyed Ezili," a minor god.

EZILI-COEUR NOIR—"Black hearted Ezili."

ERZULIE—Goddess of home and purity.

EXEMAN—God of rain and rain-making.

FONGHE—Designates the genii, good or bad. Inferior to Mawu.

GBO—"Mars," protector of the brave and enemy to the coward.

GENERAL FOUILLE—"General Dig." A relative of Baron-Samedi who digs graves.

GENERAL JEAN-BAPTISTE TRACE—"General John the Baptist Trace." A relative of Baron-Samedi who marks out the places for graves.

GU (or OGU)—Blacksmith of the gods. He is a warrior god, a diety of fire, power, and wisdom. He is symbolized by a sword stuck in the ground.

GUEDE—The spirits of death whose color is black.

GUEDE-NIMBO—A member of the Guede family (Baron-Samedi, Generals Trace, Dig, and others) who watches over the dead. All members of this family have powers of black-sorcery and necromancy. A Baron is depicted as an undertaker; in top hat, black suit, white gloves, starched cuffs, and a cane.

HU—"Neptune," god of the sea.

IBO—African gods of little importance.

IBO LELE—A forest god or spirit.

LEGBA—The intermediary deity through which all contact is made between man and gods. He is the phallic god of generation and fecundity, the master of the mystical barrier that separates the divine from the profane world. He is the one that must open the door for the faithful so that they can invoke other loa.

LA SIRENE—The wife of Agew-Taroyo (sea god).

LISA—Goddess of the moon, a Dahomey genii.

LOA—"God." Gods, spirits, angels, saints, deities, and mysteries.

LOCO ATTISO—A major healer and protector against evil spirits.

MAITRE CARREFOUR—Guardian of the crossroads (where cults meet to practice black-magic sorcery).

OGOUN FERAILLE—A powerful god of politics.

OGU—(or GU)—A warrior god, deity of fire, power, and wisdom.

OGU-BADAGRI—A god connected with fertility, wisdom, and prophesy.

OGU-BALINDJO—Sometimes known as a sea-god, at other times as a healer.

PETIT-JEAN-PIEDS-FINS—Johnny of the Delicate Feet, a minor god.

PETRO—A family of Voodoo gods which practice black-magic sorcery for evil purposes. These gods tend to be more aggressive, stern, and less forgiving than the rada loa.

PERFECT DUFFANT—The devil.

RADA—"Sun," the royal rite of the sun, a major ritual. The rada loa represent the stable, protective, benign aspects of the powers and are the most benevolent gods.

SHANGO—The War God.

SIMBI—A family of gods associated with watery places.

SOGBO—God of the lightning.

ZAKA—(or Papa Azzaca). The guardian and protector of agriculture. He is often called "Cousin Zaka" and is depicted similarly to our scarecrow, a peasant-like form.

ZO—God of fire and protector from fires.

A complete list of Voodoo gods would be impossible to compile. New gods are constantly being introduced and old ones forgotten. The gods' form and characteristics are continually being modified and changed.

ERSULIE'S BOAT by which the initiate is taken to Ife.

DICTIONARY OF WORDS and TERMS

A

ACONS—A gourd rattle, usually decorated with beads for ceremonial use.

AFRICAN Malinke-Bambara chant:
"A large pain, a great pain,
A small pain, a big pain!
Growing there and growing here,
Growing slowly everywhere!

AKATHASO—Evil spirits which inhabit trees.

AMULET—Something carried or worn for protection against danger, evil spirits, loss of property, nightmares, black magic sorcery, or for good luck, to gain love, etc. May be a stone, gem, ring, or other symbolic possession made of hide, metal, or clay. The Voodooist carries an "ouanga" bag.

ANOINTING OILS—Witches usually anoint their altar and their bodies before invoking spirits. The oils are compounded by one who believes in magical powers and the ingredients are a closely guarded secret.

APHRODISIAC—Having the power to stimulate sexual desire or excitement; often produced by an "ouanga" bag, exotic perfume, or certain foods and herbs.

ARBRES-RESPOSOIRS—Sacred trees that grow near temples.

AUTO-ZOBOP(Tiger-car)—A ghost-car driven by the "zobop" cult. They drive by night and the lights beam a blue streak.

B

BAGI—A room at the far end of a houmfo (temple). It is an altar and contains all the objects used at a ritual ceremony—bells, thunderstones, gourd rattles, voodoo dolls, pots for the captured spirits, a sword (for Gu), candles, offerings for the gods, etc.

BAKA—Evil spirits.

BAMBOCHE—A party or feast.

BARRIERE—The gate through which one hopes to enter the ecstatic trance-like state of the spirit world and become "possessed."

BENOIT BATRAVILLE, GENERAL—Commander of caco revolutionary forces, killed in 1920. His followers believed he was a bocor (a sorcerer of the culte des morts) but he was known by others to be a devout Catholic. After his death, a booklet of secret formulas for black magic was found on his body, written in Creole and in his handwriting.

BILLIS—African witches who are capable of preventing the growth of crops.

BITABAS—An African witch-doctor.

BIZAGO—A modern Voodoo cult of black magic and evil doings.

BLACK MAGIC—Sorcery with an evil purpose. Witchcraft with destruction or harm intended to the victim.

BLACK MASS—Sacrilege. To worship the devil and blaspheme God with obscenities. The cult of the devil is known to turn the crucifix upside-down and recite the credo backwards!

BLACK SORCERY—The vile practice of casting a spell, a hex, or putting a curse on some victim.

BO—Kiss.

BOCOR—A sorcerer for the "culte des morts," the cult of death.

BOHSI (or BOHLA)—A secret Dahomey password, unknown to the uninitiated.

BOKO—A sorcerer.

BOKOR—A witch that controls the spirits of the dead.

BOUTIK—A shop.

BON DIEU—A good God.

BRUIER ZIN—Voodoo initiation ceremony. At the climax, initiates are tested by putting their feet into hot anointing oil.

BRUJA or BRUJO—A Cuban witch.

BRUXA—A Portuguese sorcerer of evil.

BUNGO-BEE—A bumble bee.

C

CACO—Bad or evil.

CADEUS BELLEGARDE—A notorious papaloi turned into a pathological monster of crime and murder.

CALI—The Queen of demons who wore only robes of black and a necklace of gold skulls.

CANDLES—Rituals using candles have been prevalent since ancient times and candles have many uses and purposes in all Voodoo rituals. The forest of Haiti have been known to be ablaze with thousands of candles.

Candles provide a means for the faithful to show their devotion in a tangible manner, and they can be burned for every conceivable purpose—symbols of faith, to gain love or wealth, for health, and to cast spells and exorcise evil. It is believed various colors give off specific vibrations, such as:

WHITE—Truth, purity, spiritual strength.
RED—Love.
GOLD—Attraction, drawing, persuasive.
LIGHT BLUE—Spiritual understanding, protection, power to perceive.
GREEN—Fortune and wealth, good crops or harvest.
BROWN—Non-specific.
PINK—Success, conqueror of evil.
BLACK—Sadness, evil, mourning.
YELLOW—Dispels evil, anger, discord.
DARK BLUE—Subduing.

Those who follow the Philosophy of Fire recommend the burning of the colored candles which are in harmony with the subject. Thus, a specific astral color is recommended for each astrological sign.

The popularly accepted astral colors according to each sign are:

White—Aries
Red—Taurus and Libra
Gold—Virgo
Light Blue—Gemini
Green—Leo and Sagittarius
Brown—Scorpio
Pink—Pisces
Black—Capricorn
Yellow—Cancer
Dark Blue—Aquarius

CANDOMBLE—One of the names by which Voodoo flourishes in South America today.

CANTIQUES DE L'AME DEVOTE—"Canticles of the Devout Soul," a book of religious prayers often chanted by the Creole peasants.

CASMARAN—Magical name for summer.

CATS—The cat has always been associated with the devil, magical powers, and witches. Fear of cats is known as ailurophobia.

CAT'S EYE—A round shaped shell whose reflections resemble the eye of a cat.

CAULDRON—A pot or kettle used to brew philtres, potions, and poisons. Iron cauldrons are becoming scarce so today any bowl-like pot can be used.

CHANT—Chants are used in most cermonies to accomplish various purposes. The following one; repeated backwards, then forward, then again backwards over a sick child; is said to be a cure for worms.

Holy Monday
Holy Tuesday
Holy Wednesday
Maundy Thursday
Good Friday
Holy Saturday
Easter Sunday
Worms on the run day.

CHAT ROUGE—Red cat, a delicacy of spiced octopus—thought to be an aphrodisiac.

CHARMS—Many objects serve as charms, depending upon the symbolic significance to the individual. A powerful charm can accomplish great things, and numerous charms are sometimes required before an objective is obtained.

CHAUDIE—Pot.

CHOUAL—God's horse.

COCKCROW—Sunrise. All Voodoo rituals end at cockcrow.

CONDUI—A guide; to lead.

CONJURE—To evoke evil or good spirits to do your bidding.

CONSECRATED CANDLE–A candle which has been dressed with magical oils by one who believes in supernatural powers. One burns a candle with a specific purpose in mind, and the purpose is often written on a square of parchment and placed under the candle so that the candle's flame is directed toward a particular objective.

CONNAISSANCE–Having knowledge or skill.

CRISE MYSTIQUE–A person "possessed" by a god or spirit; having a mystical experience in a trance-like state.

COULEVRE–Snake.

CROSS-ROADS–A place where four roads join. Cults meet at night at the cross-roads for rituals.

CUI–Bake or cook.

CURSES–Misfortune or sickness brought on as the result of a hex-spell or curse; sometimes referred to as a "crossed condition." To remove a curse the sorcerer must transfer it to something more important than its possessor, and the witch must have full freedom of powers to be successful. Oils, powders, and baths are sometimes successful in "uncrossing" a person.

A typical Dahomey curse goes like this:

May your heart be rent asunder!
May your spine be split apart, and
May your ribs be torn asunder!
May your neck and head be split open!

D

DAHOMEY–A country in West central Africa on the Gulf of Guinea, a former French colony.

DAMBALLAH–Snake god. The most important Voodoo god, symbol of the universe.

DANGBESI–African priestess who serves the cult in the temples of Dangbe.

DEATH–Death concerns the mysterious and the immortal. In Brazil the dead are guarded from demons. It is believed that the ringing of a bell, of its own accord, is a sign of approaching death.

DEGOUTANT—Disgusting.

DEMON—A servant of the devil determined to destroy.

DERANGE—Disturb or annoy.

DEMONIAC—A person possessed by an evil spirit. Facial swelling, grimaces, staring, insensitivity, twitching, and leprosy are thought to be signs of a demoniac person.

DEPENSE—Spend.

DEPOSE—To put down or lay down.

DEVIL—General name for a demon. In Africa natives put bread on the ground for the devil (evil spirits).

DIVINATION—To gain knowledge of the unknown or future by conjuring up spirits. This is done by astrology, palmistry, crystal-gazing, handwriting, tarot cards, etc.

DOCTEURS-FEUILLES—Herb doctor.

DOGS—Dogs are often companions to sorcerers. The devil can take the form of a dog in order to follow a witch about unrecognized. In Ethiopia the dog is regarded as a king.

DOVE'S BLOOD—A scarlet red ink used for writing.

DRAGON BLOOD BATH—Recommended to obtain faith, constancy, the spirit of success, and to attract attention. About one teaspoonful is used in the bath water, either alone or in combination with other oils.

DOLLS—One of the best-known forms of magic is that of working through a doll to represent a person. Dolls can be of wax, cloth, straw, or almost any material. Wax dolls are often tossed into a fire to burn to complete the spell. Any doll used should be tagged with the name of the person it is to represent, and some item belonging to that person (a piece of clothing, a bit of hair, fingernail clippings, or a photograph) should be attached to the doll to make the spell or hex more effective. Whether the doll is used to gain love or to destroy an enemy, the person the doll represents should be made aware that the doll is being used and the purpose of the spell being attempted.

The hex spell is created for protection from harm or an enemy, and if a curse has been put on a person it must be un-hexed by employing a more powerful witch to transfer the evil spell back onto the enemy or evil spirit. A doll is used to symbolize the person or spirit and is bound with a red cord to represent the life-line. The sorcerer shouts out the hex curse while pulling the red cord tighter and tighter. Then a pin or needle is stuck into the doll, generally in the region of the liver. The spell is now cast. Repeat the ritual every day for nine days or until the wish has been granted.

There are rituals and magic to carry out every evil or self-seeking purpose; to cause injury or death, to obtain riches, to bring bad luck to enemies and rivals, or good luck and love to the petitioner. The doll has no magical powers alone, but concentration, suggestion, and auto-suggestion are powerful magic.

Dolls are often made in particular colors to accomplish specific objectives, and the color symbology most generally accepted is red for love, black for hate, green for luck and money, pink for success, and yellow to dispel evil forces.

DREAMS–Thought to be visitations from demons or spirits. To interpret dreams much skill and knowledge is required.

DROITE–Right.

DUPPY–Term for ghost in demonology.

E

EN AVANT–Ahead or forward.

EFFIGY–A stuffed image of a hated person. In Voodoo life-sized heads of wood or lead are sometimes used.

EN RETARD–Late.

ENIGMA–A baffling or perplexing problem; a riddle or a saying.

EVIL EYE–The power to harm others by staring hypnotically.

EXORCISM–To expel evil demons from persons or places by spells, incantations, or conjuration.

F

FANCY ANNA–Creole term for a red blossomed poinciana tree.

FARLAS—Magical name for autumn and winter.

FETISH—Any object regarded to have magical powers. Articles used by others that produce aphrodisia. There are both protective and destructive fetishes, and it is a vital part of Voodoo practice to have a garment or an article belonging to the person one is attempting to harm, control, or compel in any way.

FIXE—Fix.

FLOOR WASH—Friday is the best day to wash the floors of your home. There are several floor washes (Chinese Wash, Van Van, etc.) which can be added to the scrub water to encourage friendly spirits in the home and to discourage evil forces.

G

GALPOT—A black-magic cult.

GARTER—An emblem of rank among witches. All witches wear a garter, and men wear them on the arms. Parisian garters are worn for protection against evil spirits.

GLACE—Mirror or ice.

GODE—To store or keep; look at.

GRAND-GOU—Hunger or appetite.

GOAT-WITHOUT-HORNS—A person intended for sacrifice.

GOVI—The sacred serpent.

GRIFFE—A brown-skinned Creole, between black and mulatto.

H

HAIR—Witches offer their hair to the devil when making a pact. Bits of hair from a subject are very powerful charms when attempting a hex-spell.

HERBS and ROOTS—Man has carried herbs and roots as amulets, charms, and talismans since Biblical times. Moses, Egyptian priests, the ancient Romans, Greeks, Celts, Druids, Arabs, and others knew of the magic power of herbs.

Many persons carry herbs and roots for protection from evil, and others believe that they can heal, bring good fortune, arouse a lover, bring back a wandering husband or wife, and make wishes come true. All Voodooists carry a wide assortment of herbs to cover any difficulty, circumstance, or emergency.

ACACIA–Of great help in psychic development.

ADAM & EVE ROOT–A pair is used to hold the love of wife, husband, or sweetheart–one carried by both parties.

ANGELICA ROOT–The "Root of the Holy Ghost." Tends to prolong life.

ASH TREE LEAVES–A talisman of good luck.

BALM GILEAD BUDS–Mends a broken heart, and tempers the fires of love.

BASIL–A divine herb which brings protection to every part of the body, and brings children to those who desire them.

BETONY–Gives relief from toothache.

BLACK SNAKE ROOT–To soften a lover's heart.

BLOOD ROOT–Used in many love spells and philtres.

CLOVER TOPS–Carried as a charm against snakes, poisonous creatures, witches, and for breast complaints of women.

CLOVES–Worn to comfort the heart and bring solace to the sad.

CORIANDER SEED–Has been used as a stomachic and carminative.

CUMIN SEED–Give these to a lover to keep him, or her, faithful.

DAMIANA LEAVES–Aphrodisiac qualities are attributed to these.

DEVIL'S BIT–Worn around the neck to drive away evil spirits.

DILL–Carried to counteract any spells caused by witches or sorcerers.

DRAGON'S BLOOD REED–Carried as an aid in uncrossing a person.

ELDER BARK–For curing toothache, quieting nerves, and keeping the home from all attacks.

ELECAMPANE ROOT–Powerful aid in affairs of the heart.

EUPHORIA HERB—For maintaining a calm manner and cool disposition.

FIVE-FINGER GRASS—Wards off any evil that five fingers could bring.

FLAX SEED—Promotes peaceful relations in the home.

FRANKINCENSE—Used in many religious and spiritual ceremonies.

GRAINS OF PARADISE—Carried in the purse or pocket as a sexual stimulant.

HEART'S EASE—A sacred herb considered a talisman of love.

HOLY HERB—Concentrate while steam is rising from the tea made of this to carry one's thoughts to a higher spiritual plane and to call up the spirits.

HYSSOP LEAVES—Before and after casting spells, wash the hands in brew made with this herb.

JOHN THE CONQUEROR ROOT—Carried to insure victory in battle and against all odds.

KOLA NUTS—Soothing to the nerves.

LAVENDER FLOWERS—An aid in drawing one's lover nearer.

LIFE EVERLASTING LEAVES—A charm against illness and to lengthen life.

LOTUS ROOT—Encourages pleasant thoughts and memories, and discourages despondency.

LOVAGE ROOT—Carried near the heart to attact a lover.

MAIDEN HAIR—Brings grace, beauty, and love to those who secret a bit near the heart.

MANDRAKE ROOT—(or Ginseng). Also known as "The Root of Life" or as "The Divine Root." Believed to rejuvenate and to be an aphrodisiac. A sorcerer holds this root in one hand when creating a spell. The shape of this valuable plant has a striking resemblance to a human figure in its whole form; a small knot at one end for a head, then a thicker "body," and two thinner ends for legs. A whole root is difficult to obtain, and said to be worth its weight in gold—selling for hundreds and even thousands of dollars.

MARJORAM—Prized as a charm against witchcraft, for no one who has sold their soul to the devil can abide the odor.

MISTLETOE—A remedy against fits, witches, and to insure love and devotion.

MOJO WISH BEAN—Make a wish on this bean for nine days, then toss the bean into water to make the wish come true.

MULLEIN LEAVES—Used by witches and wizards in their incantations. Also considered a love charm.

MUSTARD SEED—Symbol of faith and to insure beautiful children.

MUGWORT—A cure for gout and for fevers.

MYRRH—Used in many sacred ointments and oils. Used in the purification of women as ordained by Jewish law.

NUTMEG—Carried for gambling luck. If a hole is bored into the nutmeg, filled with mercury, and sealed with wax, the nutmeg will take on exceptionally lucky powers.

ORANGE FLOWERS—An early and happy marriage is assured if a young maiden secrets these petals beneath her pillow.

ORRIS ROOT—The "love root" which is used to bring love between two people when given to one by the other.

PASSION FLOWER—Carried to increase the passions of whoever is nearby.

PATCHOULY LEAVES—Known as "Graveyard Dust." Mix with things of evil and bury far away from home.

PERIWINKLE—Will cause love to arise between a man and woman when sprinkled on both person's clothes.

PEONY—Carried for good luck in all matters.

POPPY—Insures peaceful sleep, and aids in assuaging grief.

QUEEN'S ROOT—Carried by those who wish to attract the attention of the opposite sex.

ROSE BUDS—These should be sewn into a bag and left in a drawer until Christmas. Then take the bag from the drawer and wear it in the bosom—the next young man one meets will become a lover or husband.

ROSEMARY—Strengthens memory and the heart, and signifies loyalty, devotion, and love.

RUE—Makes the wits more alert and prevents maids from going wrong in affairs of love. Also, an antidote for poison.

SACRED BARK—Carried as a protection against witchcraft and hex spells.

SEA LETTUCE—A small bit kept in a narrow bottle with alcohol and placed near a window will insure prolonged good luck in the home.

SLIPPERY ELM—Will help cure abscess when applied to the infected area.

SOLOMON SEAL—Carried for health and long life.

SANDALWOOD—Carry for good luck. Burn for a fragrant incense.

ST. JOHN'S BREAD—One who carries this seed pod will never go hungry.

ST. JOHNSWORT HERB—Hang over the bed to dream of your future mate.

SUMBUL ROOT—Worn near the heart to attact good luck and ward off diseases.

VALERIAN ROOT—Restores peace between combatants, and induces harmony between husband and wife.

VERVAIN—Wish on this herb, and every wish will come true.

VETIVERT—A love root and conductor of peace and contentment.

VIOLET—Breaks down the barriers of indifference, aids in the reunion of lovers and in marital problems.

WAHOO BARK—Commonly used in uncrossing a person. Make a tea of this and while rubbing it on the head, call "Wahoo" seven times very quickly.

WORMWOOD—Alleviates and prevents female troubles.

YARROW—Brought to weddings to insure seven years of love and happiness.

HEX (or HEXERAI)—To bewitch or jinx, something to create bad luck.

HEX-DOCTOR—A witch doctor who does black magic and casts hexes on victims.

HORSESHOE—Traditional charm for good luck. Actual horseshoes are hung over a door to bring good luck into the home and, contrary to most common usage, the two points of the shoe should be upward. This is believed to hold in the luck which is drawn into the shoe. If it is hung with the open end downward, the luck will come, but will pour out almost as quickly.

Small-sized horseshoes, and magnetized ones, are carried in the purse, pocket, or ouanga bag to attract good luck.

HOUGAN—A priest or priestess who is the official director at a Voodoo rite.

HOUMFO—Temple where rites are held. Any ordinary hut may serve as a houmfo.

HOUNGENIKON—The person who directs the chants and dances at a Voodoo ceremony.

HOUNSI—Servants of the gods. They assist the Hougan and are chosen from the "kanzo"—those fully initiated into the cult. They usually perform as dancers or singers of chants at ceremonies, and must be baptized before they can obtain this grade.

HUMMINGBIRDS—In Mexico a young man will wear a dead hummingbird around his neck to feel that he is attractive to many women.

I

IFE—"City of camps," symbolizing paradise lost—the end of the journey by initiation into the cult.

INCENSE—The first known recipe for incense is given in the Bible—Exodus, Chapter 30, Verses 34 through 36—wherein Moses was given a recipe. The Chinese have always employed incense when consulting the Gods and in magical rites. Today incense is used by those who wish the spiritual and occult power which will enable them to invoke any spirit they desire. Many burn incense for specific petitions—to gain affection, secure friendships, for success in business, or to safeguard themselves against enemies and evil forces.

A few of the most popular incenses are:

ATTRACTION—The odor seems to have the ability to attract the senses and sweep the mind into pleasing thoughts.

COMMANDING—Best results are obtained when the powerful incense is pressed tightly in the right hand before burning, and the names of those to be commanded are repeated nine times, each time adding the words "Allah Aye Allah Shimalah."

COMPELLING—The names of those one wishes to compel should be written on parchment and the parchment placed under the incense burner, calling the names seventeen times while the incense is burning.

HELPING HAND—Burned for various pleas of assistance, particularly to control evil spirits which may hound one.

JINX REMOVING—For use in removing crossed conditions, hex-spells, and curses which may have been cast upon a person or a place.

JOHN THE CONQUEROR—Burned to eliminate any forces which work against one. Make sure the smoke reaches every corner of the house to absorb good vibrations and insure that friends will enter with cheerful face.

INCUBUS—A male spirit which has intercourse with mortal women.

J

JINX REMOVING SALT—A black salt-like substance which is to be sprinkled in front of the house or place of business. Place this outside so that persons entering will walk on it or over it without noticing it and evil forces will not be brought into the home or store.

K

KAY-Hut.

KOB—A cent or penny.

L

LA-PLACE—A sort of master of ceremonies at a Voodoo ritual who introduces the events.

LA PLI—Rain.

LE CULTE DES MORTS—A Voodoo necromancy cult which employs the use of corpses for magical purposes.

LED—Ugly.

LITANY (or Chant)—The papaloi shouts a line, and the cultists repeat it, over and over again until another line is shouted. A typical one is:

Do not flood us with rain!
Do not set fire to my house!
Do not kill my horse!

LODESTONE (or Loadstone)—A magnetic rock which is carried to attract all the good influences toward the one who is carrying the lodestone. Some persons believe lodestones should be carried in pairs—one to repel evil and the other to attract good luck. Natural lodestones are black, but painted ones are sometimes available in a choice of colors—white, red, green, blue, etc.

LOIN—Distant; away.

LOILOICHI—A wild frenzy-like stomach dance which is performed at ceremonies in West African rituals.

LOUPS-GAROW—Werewolves.

M

MACOUTE—Straw suitcase.

MACUMBA—One of the names by which Voodoo flourishes today in South America.

MADAME SARA—A crow, or woman peddler.

MAGIC—A mysterious, inexplicable effect for which there is no natural or scientific explanation; hence, sorcery caused by supernatural sources.

MAGIC CIRCLE—The circle within which a witch stands in order to be protected from harm while evoking the spirits.

MAGICIANS—A sorcerer, or witch, who produces magical happenings. They discover dark secrets, heal by closely guarded formulas, and many times can do prophecy.

MAGNETIC SAND—An attraction sand for good luck at games and in gambling, available in gold or silver. Sprinkle in front of the home to attract friends and lovers, sprinkle in front of a place of business to attact customers and money.

MAMALOI (or MAMBO)—An old woman who has a good reputation for witchcraft.

MANDRAGORA—A plant of the nightshade family to which the mandrake belongs. Often used synonymously for the mandrake.

MANGERS—Sacrifices of animals and offerings of food made to a loa (gods) during a ceremonial rite.

MANGER-LOA—Feeding the loa to gain favor and have sins forgiven.

MARINETTE-BWA—CHECH—Marinette of the dry arm, a minor Voodoo god.

METALS—Almost all metals contain magical properties. Iron is a protection against the evil-eye. Copper contains sulphur, a healing element.

MINERALS—Magical, curative, and supernatural qualities are attributed to many rocks, gems, and precious stones. In order for a mineral to serve as an effective charm it must come in physical contact with the person, it cannot simply be in the same house or room, but should be carried either in pockets of the clothes one is wearing, or placed in a suitable bag or pouch and pinned to the garments close to the body. It is by touching the stone that the most effective vibrations are aroused.

AETITES—An eaglestone. Prevents abortion when worn bound to the arm.

AGAPIS—Dip in water and rub over the wound to cure stings and bites from venomous animals.

AGATE—The best stone for healing serpent or scorpion bites.

AMBER—An aid to furthering ambitions, and for healing throat disease.

AMETHYST—Often called the Stone of Venus. A most potent gem. It assists those who wear it to maintain faithfulness, gives the wearer the gift of tongues, the ability to prophesy, and wards off drunkenness.

AQUAMARINE—Assists the inspiration, and is favorable for travelers as it helps to protect against accidents. Also it is a powerful aid to happiness in marriage.

BALASIUS—Tends to help liver disorders, and to relieve infirmities in eyes.

BERYL—A stone, very hard and lustrous, which should be worn as a protection against evil and gossip and rumor. Also a good medium for magical vision.

BLOODSTONE—A favorite for healing and strength. Soldiers of old wore it in battle, believing it had the power to stop bleeding. A talisman for warding off all accidents and disease, especially suitable for men.

CARBUNCLE—Worn to increase the feeling of self-confidence and the ability to fight through difficulties.

COPPER—For good luck and good health, a copper bracelet should be worn by both men and women. Especially helpful in preventing or curing arthritis.

CORAL—It promises a long and happy married life, protects a child from evil influences, and safeguards the teenager during the highly emotional period.

CORNELIAN (or Carnelian)—Called the Wish Stone, it is highly favorable to health, long life, and good fortune. Its special virtue is the fulfillment of one's wishes if the stone is worn near the heart.

CRYSTAL—An aid in making the wearer capable of producing visions.

DIAMOND—A symbol of bravery and strength, and also one of the emblems of innocence. An antidote against pestilence.

EMERALD—Worn by a woman it helps her to attract a true love, and worn by a man will attract a loving wife. Also an excellent preservative against decay, arrests dysentery, and heals bites from venomous animals.

GARNET—Wards off inflammatory diseases, and promotes a healthy and cheery disposition. Will insure constancy in friendship and love, preserve health, and is generally fortunate.

JACINTH, or Hyacinth—Renders the wearer extremely fascinating and strengthens the heart. Used for melancholy.

JADE—A most sacred stone and a symbol of divine revelation. Will bring good fortune and health to its owner.

JASPER—Worn to safeguard one's personal independence, and is said to bring inspirational warnings when there is danger of unfair domination from others. To aid and comfort during periods of female distress one stone is worn about the neck and another around the waist.

LAPIS LAZULI—A very hard, opaque stone much prized for its prophetic virtues. Edgar Cayce writes of this gem.

LIGNITE—Should be bound about the head to restore lost senses and to stop nose bleed.

MALACHITE—Often called a magic stone, favorable for travellers, missionaries, and other adventurers. This stone supposedly has equal amounts of negative and positive forces, thereby adding to the balance of physical and spiritual life. Helps one to achieve a fourth dimension, according to Edgar Cayce.

MOONSTONE—An aid in bringing forth memories of past lives, and also carried as a good luck piece. Sometimes called the Queen of the Heavens stone.

MOSS AGATE—Assists in the making and keeping of friends, and is helpful to farmers and all those interested in growing plants.

ONYX—Preserves against the bites of snakes and venomous insects, and assists in bringing marital happiness. When certain persons wear it, it may bring on terrible shapes to a dreamer, from which the future can be divined.

OPAL—An unlucky stone which can interfere with love and marriage unless one was born between September 23rd and November 21. To these people, it will give second sight, or clairvoyance, and prevent contagion from the air.

PEARLS—Worn as a necklace, they make the wearer chaste. A very lucky stone for those born in June.

ROSE QUARTZ—A semi-precious stone to be worn or carried for love, fidelity, peace, and a happy marriage.

RUBY—The stone of freedom, charity, dignity, and divine power. Helps to banish grief for those in mourning.

RUTILATE—Carried by gamblers and those playing games, to attract money, luck, and wealth.

SAPPHIRE—An amulet against gruesome happenings and fears. Can aid in curing mental disorders.

SARDONYX—A good luck stone for all. More potent when engraved with the head of an eagle.

SILVER—Apply to the afflicted area to help cure skin disease.

TOPAZ—Will make melancholy vanish when worn or carried in the left hand. Also wards off rheumatic troubles.

TURQUOISE—Helps ward off danger and clears one's path of pitfalls. It is unwise to wear a turquoise formerly worn by one who has died.

UNIKITE—A healing stone as well as an aid in business success.

MIRACLE—A magical feat produced by a sorcerer who preys upon innocence and gullibility. Any event that apparently contradicts the known scientific laws.

MISER—Poverty.

MONEY—Money payments from the devil will be counterfeit.

MORTALITE—A mortality; announcing death.

MYALISM—Conversing with dead spirits—a Voodoo practice.

N

NAIL CUTTINGS—Voodooists collect their nail clippings in a bowl and then burn them. This is to prevent the clippings from falling into evil hands to be used in fetishes or spells prepared against them.

O

OBAYIFO—Ashanti name for witch.

OBEAH—A Voodoo black-magic cult. It is believed that corpses were employed in their rituals.

OBEAH STICK—A staff decorated with serpents or a human head, these were used by the Obeah cult. Sometimes called The Staff of Moses, these sticks are carried by those who regard it as a symbol of power or a good luck talisman. The custom of carrying such sticks was brought to the New World in the slave ships early in the 19th Century by Medicine Men from Africa. The sticks apparently originated among the inhabitants of West Africa, or, as some believe, something similar to the stick can be traced back to the time of Moses.

According to legend, Moses had only to raise this staff to bring about his miracles—turning water to blood, or bringing on the plague of flies or darkness. From this it is easy to understand that modern man might believe that such a staff helps them overcome obstacles, control enemies, and protect one from all harm.

Many who own such sticks dress it regularly with Power Oil, believing that this regenerates the wood and the staff's supernatural powers.

The sticks serve as walking sticks as well as being used for magical purposes. When one has an enemy, the owner of an Obeah Stick simply clutches his cane by the head and points the other end at the foe, stating calmly but forcefully, "The wrath of God will be upon the one who harms me." The enemy will be in mortal fear of the stick and will turn away from his evil intentions.

It is claimed that "the ghost is on" anyone at whom the Obeah Stick is pointed.

If one has had the ghost placed upon him, there is supposedly only one way to "take off the ghost." This is done by clearing a table in the home and placing upon it a glass of rum so that the ghost can drink it and be disoriented the next morning when the remainder of the ritual is performed. Anoint the face and hands with Uncrossing Oil. Then place some Uncrossing Powder in the palm of the hand. Then blow the powder around the premises, first to the North, then to the South, to the West, and finally to the East. This clears the person and the room of all evil. Then burn a white candle until it is completely consumed.

OILS—An important part of most magical spells are compounded oils containing aromatics, fragrant extracts, and spices which are prepared by occultists and consecrated to do certain works. Many people are sensitive to the vibration of odor and color, and special oils are created to vibrate toward a specific desire. The names given to these oils and essences are the impression that has been received from their fragrance and the thoughts they have evoked in the mind of the one who prepared the perfumes.

Oils are used to anoint the body, as a perfume, to consecrate rooms or homes, as an additive to baths, for blessing objects, dressing candles, and other such purposes.

Some of the oils available, and their intended purposes, are:

ATTRACTION OIL—Ancient magicians added a bit of this oil to their bath once every seven days. Today, landlords use it on the woodwork of a house or room they wish to rent—always rubbing into the room, never outwards. The oil can be rubbed on a tree, or the wood of a tree, meanwhile calling out the name to be attracted or the wish to be fulfilled.

BEND OVER—Often put on one's clothing and body to help influence people to your will.

BLACK ART—The person who desires to bind themselves to the devil anoints their body, and their sleeping abode, with this evil oil. To jinx, hex, or cross others, a person sprinkles some where the innocent person they are scheming against will walk on or step upon this oil so their shoes, stockings, or bare feet will pick up the scent.

BLACK CAT—Add five drops to the bath water to attract the spirit of love and help gain one's desires.

CLEOPATRA—Certain odors have profound aphrodisiac properties upon people who inhale them. Many sporting people (men and women) use this oil as a perfume—rubbing it upon a spot behind the ears, between the fingers, and underneath the arms. Also very valuable when five drops are placed upon each corner of one's bed.

COMPELLING—Anoint the body with this oil. Then repeat Psalms 12, 14, and 32, and others tend to do anything you desire them to do. Use on hands, arms, and neck to attract friends.

COMMANDING—Used on body or clothes to get others to do one's bidding.

CONCENTRATION—Great spiritualists anoint themselves with this and form a trinity by rubbing upon the forehead, the feet, and then palms of the hands. Remain in darkness and silence for at least fifteen minutes after the anointing. These ministerings are an aid to raising oneself to a higher plane for proper concentration.

FAST LUCK—Rub on the hands before playing any game for money.

HIGH CONQUERING—Legal papers are often wetted at each corner with this oil and prayed over. Anoint the body for the purpose of conquering an evil or crossed condition or a spell.

HOLY—Used to anoint the body by those desiring to gain spiritual strength.

JOCKEY CLUB—Anoint wrists and ankles to get rid of evil spirits.

JOHN THE CONQUEROR—Used as a perfume to control and conquer trouble, problems, and discord.

KING SOLOMON OIL—King Solomon of Jerusalem is said to have used this anointing oil to commune with the infinite and draw upon it for tremendous wisdom and power. Can be also added to Water of Notre Dame and kept in the home to get uncrossed.

LAVENDER—Add a few drops to bath water to help gain friends.

LOVE DROPS—To attract the attention of the person you choose to be your lover, put one drop each on your ear lobes and inside each elbow.

LUCKY NINE MIXTURE—Sprinkle three drops on your clothes each day to keep your spirits gay and cheerful.

LUCKY PLANET—For those engaging in games of chance, their money and their hands should be anointed before leaving home so that the Goddess of Luck can float between the aroma on the person and the money.

MAGNET—Used to anoint candles and to attract money. Also, use as a perfume on the neck and throat so that one will have the power of talking to customers so they will buy your goods.

MASTER—Sprinkle three drops on your Ouanga Bag at the rise of each new moon, and say the following prayer:

Oh good Lord, make me stout of heart.
Oh good Lord, let my words be harkened to.
Oh good Lord, drive the evil spirit from me.
Oh good Lord, give me success.
Oh good Lord, let my sight penetrate the innermost things.
Oh good Lord, give me power to speak.
Oh good Lord, never leave me.

POWER—Anoint the head for better concentration and deeper meditations. Especially for spiritualists and mediums.

ROSE OF CRUCIFIXION—For those who desire to guard themselves against evil and the forces of black art, and to render themselves immune to crossed conditions, use this on forehead each evening at bedtime.

ROSEMARY—Add to a small bowl of water and place on the floor of each room to encourage harmony in the home.

SPIRIT—From time immemorial, one wishing to communicate with a spirit (either of a dead person or alive) would anoint themselves with an oil consecrated for the reception of Spirit Forces. It is important that the Spirit Oil be washed off the body promptly so that the aroma and vibration of this oil is not carried on the person after spirit communion is over.
Used by all who wish to be strong spiritually. Anoint the head with this oil, light a white candle, and meditate for fifteen minutes before going out into the public or about your daily tasks.

SQUINT DROPS—Wear as a perfume, or sprinkle on a letter to a husband or lover so that he will have eyes only for you and cannot see the charms of other women.

SUCCESS—Merlin, magician to King Arthur, first compounded this oil from rare and ancient flowers and consecrated it to bring success to those who use it. Today it is rubbed on currency, homes, and money containers.

TEMPLE—A creation of Oracle Craftsman, to be rubbed on the woodwork of homes, churches, or schools. Wherever this is used, psychic power and concentration is aided.

UNCROSSING—Use for seven days, either on the body or in the bath, to get rid of a crossed condition.

VAN VAN—The benefits of this oil are numerous. It is used in many spells, particularly those for attracting friends or lovers. It can be added to your floor wash to insure a friendly, pleasant home. To bring back a lost lover, put three drops on the clothes each day for fifteen days, and two drops a day thereafter.

TEN COMMANDMENTS—This was, according to legend, used to anoint the Ten Commandments plaque. Letters from certain people and one's clothing should be dressed with this oil.

VERBENA—To help bring back a mate who has left home, mix ten drops of Verbena Oil with ten drops of Rosemary Oil and add to the scrubbing water with which the floors are washed. It is best to do this on Saturdays.

OLD COINS—Some of these possess curative properties if carried close to the body.

OMENS—Signs or symbols predicting some future event. These are interpreted by secret codes and formulas.

ON—A magical word used by sorcerers to conjure.

OU—You.

OUANGA BAG—A small bag which is carried or worn about the neck for luck, to gain love, or for protection from evil spirits and harm. They are filled with an assortment of objects—all of symbolic significance—such as luckstones, feathers, a metal, sea shell, cross, candle, pair of needles, or piece of hair. For specific objectives, the bags are sometimes anointed with the proper oil.

ORISON—A prayer.

P

PAPALOI—An old man who has gained a reputation for being an expert witch. He often officiates at Voodoo cult ceremonies, invokes spirits, and is able to cast spells.

PARCHMENT—The skin of an animal, usually a sheep or a goat, prepared as a surface for writing or painting. Used in many spells, it is written on and placed under candles so that the wax from the burning candle will fall on the parchment and the petition written on it.

PARCHMENT PAPER—A fine paper having a resemblence to pure skin parchment. This is often used as a substitute for the more expensive parchment skin.

PARE—Prepare; ready.

PEACE WATER—A preparation to be sprinkled in every corner of the home to promote peace and harmony within. To attract another person to you, or to cool their anger toward you, sprinkle some of this in front of their house so that they will step on it or over it when leaving home.

PE—The altar.

PERSECUTION—To avoid, carry an orison, a small cross, and a bit of sheeting with you at all times.

PIPI—A cup-bearing cultist. One who serves drinks at a sabbat ceremony.

PLACAGE—Common-law marriage in Haiti. The wife is a "placee" and enjoys all the privileges of matrimony without an official wedding.

PLAISIRS—Pleasures; joys, delights.

POTEAU-MITAN—The center post which supports the roof of a temple. It is used as a ladder by the spirits to descend and ascend in the temple, and is usually decorated with designs.

POTS-DE-TETE—Pots or jugs which contain the initiate's soul.

POWDERS—Various powders are used as sachet, body powder, for blowing, or for sprinkling The powders can be inclosed in small sacks and placed with lingerie, clothing, or stationery. They are preferred by some over the oils or essences as the odor is not as strong and the user can never be considered "loud" or vulgar for using too much as is possible with oils.

Some of the most popular powders available are:

ALGIERS—Dust the body daily for successful love and financial dealings.

ATTRACTION—Apply to the body after bathing to help develop happiness and gain friends.

COME TO ME—Use on the bosom and neck to attract a lover.

CONFUSION—Sprinkle in front of your home to confound evil spirits which may want to attack and to turn them back from whence they came.

CONTROLLING—An aid to giving one complete control over any situation and other people. Use as a sachet powder for influencing people.

DRAWING—Put on the body to attract attention. Sprinkle on letters sent to a loved one away from home.

FRENCH LOVE—Keep some in the drawer with the underthings, and use on neck and bosom to fascinate any man.

GET AWAY—Sprinkle around the outside of your home at midnight for three consecutive nights to get rid of evil forces which may want to come in. Be sure to sprinkle completely across the entrance way to home or apartment.

HOT FOOT—If one walks on this, they will become dissatisfied with their place of living and should desire to move away, so it should be sprinkled at a place where your enemy will step on it or over it.

LOVE—To entice another person toward you, sprinkle a bit in their shoes in a way so that they will not notice it. This should keep them faithful to you to the last day. Used on the skin, it will make other persons listen to your words and love to hear you when you speak.

PEACE—Sprinkle in every corner of your living room or bedroom, so that the power of the spirit of evil who controls your enemy will lose all of its strength to work against you, and there will be peace within and around you.

UNCROSSING—Rub on your chest each morning to help improve your conditions or to get uncrossed.

WAR—Place some in front of the house where an enemy lives so that they must step on it to go in or out of the house, but be careful that no one sees you put it there. The powder will tend to make your enemy so cross and contrary that his friends will not be able to abide him any longer.

The above is not nearly a complete list of powders for there are many, many others, including Altar, Business (for encouraging customers to come into your store), Double Crossing (for use if you suspect others of using evil means against you), Goofer Dust, Holy Spirit, Lucky Lady, Magnet (for fascinating and drawing friends toward you), Master, Protection (for sprinkling across your entryway so that no evil spirits can enter), Separation (to encourage lovers to get together again), Turn-A-Back, Victory, Vision, Wealthy Way, and Zodiac. Also, check list of oils as powders of the same name are generally used in a similar manner.

PROGNOSTICATIONS—Predictions or prophesy.
Examples: When great oaks bear many acorns, a long hard winter is ahead. Stars seen by day forecast a holocaust. Thunder at noon will mean rain before night.

PROVERBS—A maxim or adage.
A few Creole proverbs are: Rock in river bottom never know sun is hot. No cuss alligator's long mouth 'til you cross the river. Seven years never too long to wash speckle off a guinea hen's back.

R

RED SECTS—Secret societies, cults.

RELE—Call or shout.

S

SABBAT—A meeting of witches and cultists gathered together to perform evil doings—to cast spells and evoke spirits, to create mysteries and instill fear and fright into others.

SABBAT CHALICE—Drinking cup used at mass.

SABBAT DANCE—A dance performed to the sound of drums, flute, bead-decorated gourd rattles, and chanting.

SALT—Used as a magical ingredient in casting spells. If one is under a spell, then salt is poisonous and one must eat unsalted food.

SAUT d'EAU—Waterfall of Haiti.

SEALS—A design reproduced on metal, parchment, or paper which serves as a talisman to the person carrying or owning it. A seal should always be a secret possession and should be kept in a safe place, or worn on the person. They are often sewn into coat linings, inserted into mattresses, worn in shoes, carried in purses or pocket books, or secreted in clothes closets or drawers. The most popularly available seals are those taken from the Sixth and Seventh Books of Moses, and they are generally reproduced in Dragon Blood red ink on parchment paper.

Some of these seals, and the intended purpose, are:

SEAL OF ARIELIS—For compelling others.

SEAL OF ANTIQUELIS—For good health.

SEAL OF AZIABELIS—For achieving great power.

SEAL OF AZIELIS—For commanding power.

SEAL OF BARBUELIS—For controlling any situation.

BREASTPLATE OF AARON—Protection from sudden or violent death.

CANDALABRA SEAL—For attainment of desires through prayer and candle rites.

SEAL OF ELEVATION & SPIRITUAL REDEMPTION—To bring peace into the home and to mend broken marriages.

SEAL OF GOOD FORTUNE—Great aid in business deals.

SEAL OF GREAT FORTUNE—To be safe on and in the water.

SEAL OF GOOD LUCK AND FORTUNE—For success in games and in gambling.

SEAL OF HONOR AND WEALTH—For plentiful gold and silver.

SEAL OF INFLUENCE AND POWER—For popularity and power.

SEAL OF JESUS OF GOD—For protection in all matters.

SEAL OF JUPITER—Fortune and good luck in all endeavors.

KING SOLOMON SEAL—Guidance, wisdom, and understanding in all matters.

SEAL OF KNOWLEDGE—Through visions or dreams.

SEAL OF LOVE—To gain and hold the love of another.

SEAL OF MARS—To aid in family arguments and hold marriages together.

MASTER KEY SEAL—Help in all problems.

SEAL OF MEPHISTOPHILIS—For conquering enemies.

SEAL OF MERCURY—Assistance in seeking employment.

SEAL OF THE MOON—Powerful aid to lovers.

SEAL OF MYSTICAL ASSISTANCE—Aid in legal affairs.

SEAL OF ORION—To have wishes fulfilled.

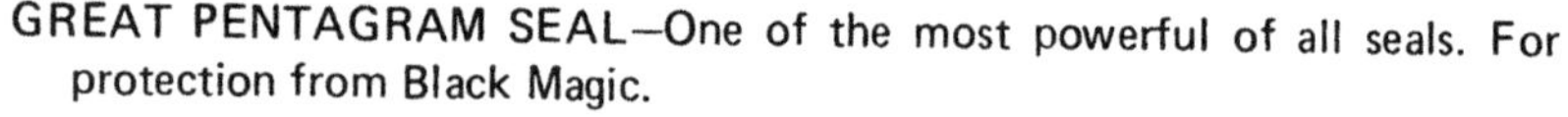

GREAT PENTAGRAM SEAL—One of the most powerful of all seals. For protection from Black Magic.

SEAL OF POWER—Magical powers are conferred to those who own and carry this seal.

SEAL OF RAB CALEB DOCTOR—For health and medical assistance.

SEAL OF RELIEF FROM WANT—For financial security and aid when seeking employment.

SCHEMHAMPHORAS HOLY SEAL—For bringing contact with departed souls.

SCHEMHAMPHORAS NO. 1 SEAL—For great success in financial and business dealings.

SCHEMHAMPHORAS NO. 2 SEAL—Highest religious seal, containing great mystical powers. To be used for good purposes only.

SEAL OF SECRETS—To prevent others from learning your confidential affairs.

SERPENT SEAL—Good health and protection from black magic.

SEAL OF SATURN—For a long life and good health.

SEAL OF SPECIAL ATTRACTION—For drawing others to you.

SEAL OF SPIRITS—For quick service and help in all desires.

SEAL OF SPIRITUAL ASSISTANCE—For help from friendly spirits.

SEAL OF TREASURE—For finding lost treasures buried in the ground.

SEAL OF TREASURES—For finding any lost or stolen article.

SEAL OF VENUS—For love and happy marriage.

SEMBLE—Similar; seem; like.

SERPENT WORSHIP—Worship of a sacred green snake which symbolizes the universe and keeps away evil spirits. This is a basic Voodoo belief.

SI DYE VLE—God willing.

SOUL—Voodooists believe that everyone has two souls, a small inferior one and a larger superior one.

SORCERERS—Persons who practice magical arts.

SORCERERS GREASE—A consecrated grease used by witches.

SPELLS—Words, formulas, or rituals supposed to have magical powers. The spell can bind, break, make, or mend; can harm an enemy, make rain, banish ghosts, or raise the spirits of the dead. The power of the spell derives from the power of the ritual followed and makes use of the alleged magical properties of various objects, oils, powders, incenses, and talismans.

Secret formulas for spells are compiled in "grimories" and are closely guarded by sorcerers. These spell books are handed down from one generation to another and assume an almost sacred character.

SPIRITS—There are inferior earthly spirits, and there are superior celestial spirits.

SPRAYS—Today there are several sprays available which are quick and efficient for use Two of the most popular are Good Luck Spray which is sprayed into each room, every corner, and including closets and cupboards to encourage a pleasant and cheerful home; and Jinx Removing Spray which is sprayed in the same places so that undesirable vibrations will find it impossible to stay. Good Luck Spray is used in the mornings, and the Jinx Removing at night or late evenings.

SYMBOLS—Basic symbols, sometimes tattoed on faces, are:

Serpent Sexual Three Paths Three Circles

Voodoo mysteries move through three circles.

T

TOMBOUR—Drum.

TCHATCHA (Cha-cha)—A gourd that rattles, or dry pods of trees.

TIRE—Shoot.

TOADS—Witches are often depicted with toads for pets. It is believed that they train the toads to obey commands and orders.

TO SUMMON THE LOAS (gods or spirits)—The high priest of Voodoo will draw a veve design (symbol of the loa) with corn meal or coffee on the grounds or floor around the center post of the temple. He then shakes a gourd rattle and shouts the name of the loa to be invoked—this is repeated over and over until the loa descends into the temple. Everyone kneels to kiss the "veve" before a ritual may begin for it will be erased by the dancing of the cultists.

TONTON—Uncle.

TREASURE-HUNTING—This is a favorite pastime of Haitians and sometimes even profitable as in colonial days pirates did bury treasure in Haiti.

TRACA—Trouble or nuisance.

TROIS-HOUSE—A hoe, a gravedigger's tool.

TROIS-PELLES—A shovel or spade.

TROIS-PICQUOIS—A pick.

TUE—Kill.

U

UBASTI—A cat goddess, represented as a cat-headed woman.

UNCROSSING baths, oils, powders, sprays—Used for seven consecutive days to remove jinxes, curses, hexes, and all crossed conditions from the user.

V

VOODOO—A body of rites and practices based on a belief in sorcery and in the power of charms, fetishes, objects, etc. Introspection of the unknown. A Voodooist believes first and then seeks to prove the belief. It is the practice of suggestion and therefore often successful—very few thinking people are immune to the powers of suggestion. Even unbelievers have been victims of Voodoo as the unconscious mind of most persons harbors fear and superstitions. Voodoo is a pantheistic religion which takes its gods and deities from old kings and gods of Guinea and the Congo, most originating from the Dahomey peoples. The concepts have affinity with many other great religions and mythologies. The titles of Papa, Maitre, and Maman are prefixed to old names of loa.

VOODOO DRUMS—There are always three drums used at rituals; all of unequal size—call maman, papa, and boula (baby).

VOODOO RITES—There are two major rituals: the RADA (Royal Rite of the Sun) which is an initiation ceremony, and the PETRO which is the dispenser of magical power rite.

In the Rada ritual an initiate becomes "possessed" by spirits and is taken to "Ife" (City of camps) where magical powers are obtained. The voyage is made in "Agwe's boat" which is guided by Erzulie, symbol of ceremonial water and dispenser of beauty, love, and health as well as hate, jealousy and vengeance. Since Erzulie is Queen of Heaven and Earth, she has two faces, both ugly and beautiful.

On the altar is placed everything needed for the ceremony—a symbol of "Damballah" is on a pedestal in the center, sabbath candles in holders are surrounded with luck stones, beads, necklaces, a crucifix, decorated gourd rattles, jugs with rum and wine. Plates are filled with cakes, bread, vegetables, eggs, and fruit. Cigars are also offered to the loa. The "ouanga" bag of a new initiate is also on the altar, and three drums are to one side of the altar.

In front of the altar, or in the center on the floor, a "hougan" or "mambo" witch draws a veve design to symbolize the loa to be called upon. If it is a sea loa they wish to conjure, water is poured in the center of the veve. The witch will now shout out the lines of a chant which all others repeat in chorus:

Papa Legba, open the gate wide!
Papa Legba, where are the children?
Papa Legba, we are here.
Papa Legba, open the gate wide so that we can pass!

Legba is the loa who can open the barrier for the faithful so they can invoke other loa.

The witch now shakes his rattle and shouts out, "Agwe, I beg you in the name of Legba to help us." Some of the chorus chant while others begin to dance. The witch calls out lines for everyone to repeat:

"Hail to Papa Agwe, who dwells in the sea,
Agwe is loa of ships!
In a blue sea, there are three small islands!
The negro's boat is in danger,
Papa Agwe bring it to safety!
Hail to Papa Agwe!"

The three Rada drums join in—everyone chants, shakes bells, rattles, or dances to the music. They seethe with emotion, ecstasy and exhaustion. Food and drink are taken to nourish body and soul.

During the ceremonies, if some become "possessed" by spirits, they are watched over and protected by the others. Jewelry and valuables are put away for safety and anything which could harm others or themselves is removed from the person. Intoxication is unheard of at a ceremony—all the emotion and frenzy is created by the spirituality of the people.

The spell has now been cast by the witch—not everyone becomes "possessed" and not everyone is initiated.

The service is most likely to be held on Saturday night since any Voodoo ritual is long and strenuous, and on Sunday the participants can sleep late and slowly recover

Funeral rites often have a bizarre quality to them. It is a festive affair and a feast is prepared. The corpse is in full formal dress and propped up at the table to participate. Jokes are told and games are played—some of the jokes relating to the deceased. The corpse is blessed by the priest and taken away by runners who carry it to the cemetery via a zig-zag path so that the soul cannot find the path back. A large, black cross with the symbol of Baron-Samedi on it is placed on the grave.

One initiatory rite is the procedure known as "laver-tete." The initiate's head is washed and covered with a paste made up of herbs, rice, bread, syrup, and blood. This is to place the novice under the protection of a particular loa who will from then on act as his personal protector.

Sacrifical ceremonial rites—stories of human sacrifice in Voodoo cults—have been rumored but no proof or evidence of this is known to exist. In the past animals have sometimes been used—usually poultry.

W

WANGA—Magic; also implies empirical medicine.

WETE MO NA DLO—A ceremony of "fishing the deceased's soul out of the water." This ceremony is used only when a dead soul strikes down a relative with some disease which can only be cured by this ritual.

WHITE MAGIC—The practice of sorcery for good and ethical purposes—for protection from harm, to gain love, to cure illness.

WITCH—A woman supposed to have magical or supernatural powers. Also, commonly used for a man also, though "warlock" is the proper term for a male witch.

WITCHCRAFT—Sorcery; the practices of witches; black magic, an irresistable influence or fascination.

WITCH DOCTOR—An herb or leaf doctor. Many of their remedies actually have a real therapeutic value.

Y

YO—They.

YOU SEUL—Single; one only.

YOUN—One.

Z

ZEGUI—Needle.

ZEPINGLES—Pins.

ZIN—Pot.

ZOBOP—A mob of sorcerers, members of secret societies devoted to magical gangsterism. Few Haitian peasants will dare go out alone at night for fear of these groups. Each region has its own names for these "red sects" (as they are collectively known)—galipotes, "hairless pigs," "grey pigs," and vlanbindingues. Among their atrocities, the peasants accuse the zobop of changing their victims into beasts which are about to be slaughtered.

ZOUTI—Tools.

ZWAZOO—Birds.

VOODOO SONGS & CHANTS

The chants used are dependent upon the loa of "family" being invoked at the ceremony. They have been handed down from one generation to another over the years and have naturally undergone changes. Almost none of the chants exist in written form although they are an important part of all rituals. Lines are repeated over and over until the desired effect has been achieved.

1. Papa Legba, open the gate wide!
   Papa Legba, where are the children!
   Papa Legba, we are here.
   Papa Legba, open the gate wide so that we can pass!

2. Save Mambo Mesire from drowning!
   On the day a leaf falls into the water is not the same day that it will sink!

3. Guede Nimbo Papa!
   What you do makes you no good!
   When I am present you tell good of me.
   Behind my back you speak bad of me!
   Never, Never, speak evil of me!

4. Ayida-wedo, my serpent goddess,
   When you come, it is like a lightning flash!

5. Ybo, the time has come!
   This is the time of blood, Ybo!
   What do you bring me, Ybo?
   It is I whom you see.

6. Better you should have a man in the house,
   than you should live with your mama!
   Yes, young maiden!

7. A wild pig came to me–
   I asked, why have you come?
   "Everyone is sick at Leogane!"

   A wild bull came to me–
   I asked, why have you come?
   "Everyone is sick in the mountains!"

   A wild goat came to me–
   I asked, why have you come?
   "Everyone is sick in Africa!"

So I, who are not sick, must die!

8. Hail to Papa Agwe!
Who dwells in the sea!
Agwe is Lord of the ships.

In a blue sea
There are three small islands.
The negro's boat is in danger,
Papa Agwe brings it to safety.

Hail to Papa Agwe.

9. To sea I went, I went to fish, Agwe!
I lost the hook of my loa,
I lost the hook of my loa,
I ask you, Agwe, what am I going to eat for supper?
Small conch in the sea,
What am I going to eat?

10. Yaombe! Yaombe Cimalo!
I do good for them, Cimalo,
They do not know me!
I come to make them happy, they do bad to me!
When I arrive, Cimalo, what do you want me to bring them?

In front of the altar a "hougan" or a "mambo" will draw a design similar to that above. The forked marks represent the invisible symbols through which the loa will move. Into the circle marked earth, they pour oil, flour, and wine. Into the sky circle rum and ashes are poured, and into the sea circle they pour water. The people chant while all of this is done. Then the priest draws another design in front of the entrance to the temple—to seal it.

BARON-SAMEDI and BARON-la-CROIX—they watch over the dead.

ERZULIE: "Queen of Heaven and Earth"
Symbolized with her heart pierced with a sword
and peppered with gunpowder.

When serpents are coiled in a "V,"
design symbolizes the union of male
and female